TRUTH TABLE

poems by

Heikki Huotari

Finishing Line Press
Georgetown, Kentucky

TRUTH TABLE

ACKNOWLEDGMENTS

"Love's Lift" and "Oblique" will appear in the *Avatar Review*.
"Reentry" appeared in the *Berkeley Poetry Review*.
"Asymmetric" and "The Thing You Lift" appeared in the *Coe Review*.
"Small" and "The Tenure of the Premise" appeared in *Crazyhorse*.
"The Color of Milk and Snow" and "The Crossing" appeared in the *East Coast Literary Review*.
"Between the Walls" will appear in *Fourteen Hills*.
"Quantum Logic" will appear in *Modern Poetry Quarterly Review*.
"Upgrade" appeared in *Poetry Quarterly*.
"Crop Circle" and "One Good Reason" appeared in *The Vehicle*.
"Inhale" and" "Lullaby" appeared in *Third Wednesday*.

Editor: Christen Kincaid

Cover Art: Bryan Manaois

Author Photo: Kay Bradner

Cover Design: Elizabeth Maines

Printed in the USA on acid-free paper
Order online: www.finishinglinepress.com
also available on amazon.com

Author inquiries and mail orders:
Finishing Line Press
P. O. Box 1626
Georgetown, Kentucky 40324
U. S. A.

Table of Contents

Many thanks to Kay Bradner, Stefanie Marlis and Jennifer Woodworth for inspiring, and responding to innumerable drafts of, these poems.

Moment of Inertia

We're not done with miracles, but in between.
When we put on our turtleneck, our head gets started
up a sleeve and marching bands in uniform are diving
off the bridge of which we are the lonely troll and,
our position monitored by an accelerometer, displayed
as pinpricks on our tongue, we're carbonated, carbon-
based, a never-ending nerve and almost level, almost
human. As our center and our axis match, we're true.
We lie beneath a cloud, above reflection in a pool,
magnetically suspended and an ant, a raft of ants, of
animals and plants, cooperating, saying,
We are here for you.

Small

When the moon throws photons,
I can step down into any open grave
and when my black earth bulges, I can finally
learn to fly and when the past outgrows its planter,
I can give the future one more try.
If you take all the covers, then I'm free to find
another bed or room or house in which to sleep.
But when I'm squeezed from both sides,
painted in a corner with my back against the wall,
I can but make me small,
as in a Middle-Ages painting,
as a child with adult features,
standing on my mother's lap, and small.

The Color of Milk and Snow

Sticks to pick their sticks up, stars
and scars crisscrossing, given to
reflect on, neither transmit nor absorb
and wisdom teeth extracted, scrimshawed,
sanded, road-side signs of microscopic cubic corners,
compound eyes that shine and, happy hour long
since past, last call, and suddenly we've overstayed
our welcome and the barmaid's flipping
on and off the lights and crooning *Closing.*
You don't have to go home but you can't stay here.

The Tenure of the Premise

Sorry in advance and at the square dance,
back to back, I trade my grief and guilt for yours.
The next event will feature coloring
and spooning, spinning, chinning, tossing,
nosing or the finding, in the green grass, of an egg
and at this contest everybody wins,
as life is fair. And then there's planetary life.
A leg that's bare and barely out of bed puts on
a foot with seven toes. Now vertical,
the merrier the more, we disco on a window on the floor,
our cause is probable and in our creaky hearses,
from our mildewed hymnals,
we three sing of all things sweet and sour
and from a sea of ink an artificial chicken drinks.
Our logic takes us where we want to go
and still, through all these years,
about our central premise,
not one question has been raised.

Quantum Logic

My radius a play of chain, a turn of phrase,
my thought balloon is red and round or red
not round or round not red or neither red
nor round. My thought balloon, when tweaked
and twisted, is a poodle or a hat or both a poodle
and a hat, a tag team, alternately one a futuristic
flying fish and one a prehistoric horse.
Translucent cylinders of sloshing water,
naturally occurring Stirling engines,
in their separated shaded lanes,
as in concurrence, change their course.

Crop Circle

Every moment spawns a watershed
of dialects and rights of way and self-inflicted priests.
In every window pane the face of night,
the DNA, the little liquor bottle that we share.
They're topologically equivalent, the donut
and the coffee cup, with each a glaze
and each a glint and each a coil of steam.
There's prerecorded laughter. Trusting, faithful,
all fall back. The landing wheels, just lowered,
turn, to no avail, in air. The flying saucer spins
into a field of wheat and they have simple tools
and ropes and wires and boards tied to their feet.

Between the Walls

Between the walls were pipes and wires and I,
the statements made by nails
and trails of glowing coals and I,
the waterfall of consciousness,
and we went over in our barrels,
in our naked bankrupt's barrels,
in suspenders, staves and hoops,
and we were intricate
and octopi embracing
beak to beak
and suction cup to suction cup
with every tentacle a brain.

On Certainty

It's illegal to stop walking;
when we ask for bills you give us coins
and in the doorways of your churches
there are sprinklers that turn on at three a.m.
And will you care for us when we are clean?
As when the crash is had by equal masses
one must take the credit, one the blame,
so on the tree of knowledge
there will be low hanging fruit
and though it tastes like cardboard
it costs next to nothing.
Next to nothing,
we are bodiless and odorless
and hovering, will be untouchable
and to the higher powers, birds of prey,
we'll display poison-caterpillar colors
and to bottom feeders be,
to bottom feeders be the one true light.

More

The TV urges me to wait
because there's more.
When clowns collide
the comical atomic particles fly
off in all directions and the universe
is largely laughing matter,
known by indirect effect,
the empty exoskeleton
still clinging to the tree,
the optic nerve emerging
from the safe side of the eye.
I've put my blindfold and
my handcuffs and
my cowboy costume on.
I'm keeping score.
Because I loved you, loved
you last, there's more.

One Good Reason

An ice cream truck is playing
Mary Had a Little Lamb and all God's oats are wild,
each night the first, tomorrow God goes off to war.
I say to God,
I thought you said your Virgin Mary doesn't bite,
God says,
It's not my Virgin Mary.
Anyway it's just a nibble cause she likes you and
she wants to play.
The Virgin Mary writes,
I have your dream,
and if you want to see your dream again
you'll do exactly as I say.

Love's Lift

By the scattered feathers
and the black-tape outline you will know me,
by raised footprints of compacted snow,
and one foot in my bathtub, one in bed,
a shoe in each of two canoes,
electrified, vibrating, secret spent,
I may repent, inhaling steam and chained
to my machine through swing and graveyard
shift. Positioned on a fence post
while Delilah, laughing, drives away,
I'll stick my head and neck out, arms and legs
and pointed tail and I'll be swimming in the air.
Once loved and now of worth,
I'll pity those poor turtles still on earth.

Lullaby

Curse the darkness.
Damn the candle.
In one eye and out the other goes the light
and an hallucination turns your head
and when you stumble, drunk on love,
tattoos her name somewhere on you
and now you're sitting at the children's
table making airplanes of gray plastic
fragments and evaporating glue.

Oblique

In my cone of streetlight,
on my slanted slab of concrete,
in my wobbly shopping cart a trusting puppy
and a hubcap and an amber tail light, dreaming,
I'm some family's pants, some party's life,
and I mistake a lampshade for a hat
and when the music stops at sunrise
and I'm going nowhere on some freeway,
banners on highrises tell me if I lived here
I would now be home.

Upgrade

Born in sin, you must love someone:
you may cast the second stone.
Past lives, a body in each room
and none to blame. Another day,
another cake and teeth on necklaces
that we may hold our heads up without shame.

Inhale

Iguanas freeze and lose their grips
and fall like fruit from trees,
like bricks, and during earthquakes knees
and buildings learn to flex and breathe
and in a vortex of low pressure clowns
and clown enablers scratch and stretch
and yawn and when I die again
I'll take the spiral candles from my cake
and send my parents back to jail
and when they tell me to withdraw my wishes I'll inhale.

Wrong Fish

It's the wrong fish exactly
that I focus on when I imagine hands
and heads and necks.
I should be watching striped
or spotted gars, who congregate
where idling and smoking are allowed,
whose thumbs hook in suspenders
of their disbelief, yet unopposed,
unsupervised, they feed the feeble
flames of innocence and guilt,
the red and blue rotating lights
of less than half a block from home.

Asymmetric

At the other altar, Abelard says *I do not*.
Therefore what God has put asunder
let no man or woman join. A hammer rotates,
peen and claw and handle, in slow motion
by my window on the freeway.
When I hear a flower over one ear
means a thousand nights of bliss,
the other, come within ten feet and die,
I'll surely know which ear is which.

Worthy

Worthy is the lamb that by some act
of depraved negligence is slain.
Substantial is the pedestal on which
the one who has been injured is installed.
In view of that important person's
righteous indignation, I say,
All your grievances will be redeemed
and in the shoe with ears, the hat with tail,
the stole with head and tiny feet
you'll dance between two feather fans
eternally, your equanimity of such
the rest of us can only dream.

The Crossing

If ever there were rivers they have since
gone underground. A day away, a dry oasis,
mirage, scaffold, branch of bone,
first fish with feet, the solid salt, the sand.
And take our belts and shoes and wave us through.
Kidnapped and handed hands,
we're less an island than an island shaped by waves
and in our robes, our wedding black and white,
we're serenaded: fireflies and five sizes of guitar
and when the distance between us increases it must be
that one of us is glowing, throwing clothes off in the snow.

Tooth and Spoon

When I am bibbed and tipped and partially anesthetized
and my bicuspid's ground down to a point
and soft warm parts of you contact my face's feeling side
and posters on the ceiling tell of billows, beach,
and palm tree, stories meant for only me
and you're an optical illusion, there are two of you
in scrubs and masks and safety glasses,
in one of your four hands you hold
a mirror by the handle, like a spoon,
and in another, my new tooth.

The Thing You Lift

When the thing you lift is not
as heavy as you thought
it flies up in the air. A step
is taken from you when you step,
except what you expect to step
on isn't there. And God throws down
his bike precisely at the bottom
of the stairs and when you call
him on it, when you say,
Someone will fall,
he says, *Let them take care.*

Equilibrium

Whatever can be carried
can be carried on the head—
the bale of cardboard
or the washtub filled with fruit,
and any featherless or twisted thing
that can be cradled can be cradled
in a sling, the knot behind the neck,
and any powdered wing
almost a moth
and credible or sensible
or folded soft in cloth.

Oath

I will obey Newton's Laws today.
I swear that if I'm on some track
I'll not derail or on some rack recant.
I may consider action at
a distance, using voodoo,
body language, altering the future
or the past, but overdub, as Nixon did,
It would be wrong.
I ask that I be raptured
as the other applicants,
entangled subatomic particles
and narcissistic spinning lilies
of the field, have no such qualm.

Short Circuit

Cicadas buzz because they can't fluoresce,
so low on ozone they could be
the very definition of duress
and car alarms are tuned to my tinnitus
and where one's electrical and spherical
and musical and necessary,
any cast of thousands will suffice
and by the aces up their sleeves
and rabbits in their hats
you'll know that they're infallible, inflatable,
and they have documents by which,
for every day they've missed,
they are excused.

Subliminal

Speakers in my pillow, sing me through my sleep.
Suggest a gender. Say a grace.
In sleep-paralysis, I may expend no effort,
so undress, caress, correct me,
with your wet-paint footprints teach me
where to stand and how to dance,
then furnish me with paper tail and pin
and spin me seven times and warn me
when I'm cold and when I'm warm and have me
hold my breath and hide my eyes and count
and when you see I'm giving up, come out.

Reentry

The astronauts are sleeping, their possessions, wallets,
bullets, coins and keys on distant dressers,
carry-ons in bins above their heads.
The astronauts are sleeping in the shadow of the earth
and in their wings and in their pods and soft and warm
and white.
The astronauts are sleeping in their cars,
their carts, their cardboard boxes on concrete.
The astronauts are sleeping while I pace and while I age
and while I set the breakfast table, bowls and spoons,
and after their pajama party, having whispered,
tickled half the night, now finally they're asleep
but soon they'll be awake again and tumble with
their precious laughter down the stairs.

Heikki Huotari once lived atop a forest-fire lookout tower then attended a one-room school, the only student in the second grade. As a drafted conscientious objector, he was court-martialed for refusing to eat then intravenously force-fed. As a mathematician, he independently discovered totally tubular convex bodies. These days he commingles with butterflies and hummingbirds beside a sunlit wall of morning glories.